Putting Me First: A Woman's Guide and Journal to Intentionally Healing and Making Time for Herself.
Copyright © 2016 by Regan M. Adams

ISBN 978-0692724743

Dedication

I dedicate this book to my Lord and Savior Jesus Christ. He is an awesome Savior and His love for me is unexplainable. I thank Him for letting me be a blessing to others and I pray people are able to see my light shine and be attracted to Him. I also dedicate this book to my mother Dorothy Cohen. She is a living example of a lady and the closest thing to perfection that I know. (She hates when I say that). She has always tried to live by what she taught me and I am FOREVER grateful that she is my mom. To my mother-in-law, Brenda Sanders. You aren't just my mother-in-law, you are my friend. I want you and my mother to enjoy life as much as you can because you have given both of your lives to ensure your family is happy and taken care of. It's your time now to put yourself first. I am thankful for my biological parents, Willis and Elouise Ellis for not aborting me. Without your choice, this wouldn't be possible. I appreciate my deceased father, Loue Gene Manning, who taught me not to be scared of anything; I just didn't understand what he was talking about until now. Thank you daddy. To my right-hand friend, Cynthia Fletcher, who is a God send. Thank you for helping me develop my talents and highlight my strengths, but also for telling me when I am off track. We are rocking until the wheels fall off! And finally, to my husband Darnell and our child Kennedy. You both are the reason I started Putting Me First in the first place...literally. I love you both very much.

Table of Contents

FOREWORD

Have you ever been so busy with life that all of a sudden you stop in your tracks and wonder, "Who am I and what am I doing?" Your mind starts to reminisce over the past years and how you have spent your time. Boom, you've had a "wow" moment. You begin to realize that you're a wife, a mother, a sister, an aunt, a friend, a daughter, a church member and the list goes on. Everything you've done thus far has always been for someone else! You've been so busy making everybody else's lives comfortable but you have buried all of your desires and ambitions underneath the clutter of everybody else's to-do lists. You now realize that you have lost yourself and hardly recognize the person you have become. What do you do? How do you do anything different from what you've been doing and not disrupt your family's life? They surely won't understand. The wheels are now spinning in your mind and there's a sense of disappointment because you realize that you have not taken any time for you! The degree that you wanted to pursue, the trip that you wanted to take with your girlfriend to relax for only one weekend, or the business you wanted to start so there would be something with your very own signature have gone by the wayside. So much time has passed and you've forgotten how passionate you had been about those things. They seem to be lost! But no, wait a minute! They're not lost; they're just on the back burner and now you must be intentional in bringing them forward. This is exactly how "Putting Me First" was birthed! There was a moment of realization that my friend Regan Adams had one weekend in September of 2013, when she discovered that she had lost herself in her family. She was first a wife and then a mother, working a fulltime job. We went away to a live recording service in Atlanta and had hotel reservations with each of us having our own rooms. We had so much fun for two days being away from our 'normal lives', having the bed all to ourselves, and enjoying our special "me time!" As women, we must learn to put ourselves first, sometimes. It is our innate nature to be caregivers and it is so easy to take care of everyone and make sure that their needs are met. Often, that routine becomes permanent and we never carve out time to do the things we love to do for ourselves; we continue the ritual of meeting the needs of the family. Never think for one minute that the time we take for ourselves means that God isn't first. God should always be first because without Him, we are nothing and can do nothing.

He knew what He placed inside us while we were in the womb. According to Deuteronomy 8:18, we are charged to remember the Lord our God, for it is He who has given us power to get wealth. We were born with the potential to gain wealth and it's refreshing to know that we were born to be entrepreneurs if we want to be. We also must explore what our gifts and talents are in order to properly flow into our wealthy place. Everyone is not meant for entrepreneurship, but our gifts are used to glorify God, make us happy, and bless others in the process. This is an exciting opportunity for you to get to know who you are through the workbook feature of this book. It is the perfect tool to help you explore the real you, which has been hidden for so long. Take the time to relax and enjoy the journey as you go through this book and discover how to realign your life to include 'you'!

Cynthia Fletcher, Great friend and Purpose Midwife

Introduction

On September 4, 2013, my friends and I went on a weekend trip to Atlanta to attend a gospel concert. When we got to the concert venue, we were unable to get in because it sold out. Instead of going home, we stayed for the weekend to relax. During that weekend, I was able to rest, read, rediscover myself, and enjoy a little quiet time. It had been five years since I had been by myself to do any of those kinds of things. I was always taking care of my husband or our daughter and hadn't spent a full weekend without either of them. In addition to that, I had a full-time job and on Sundays, I was off to church. Where had 'I' gone? Who was 'I'? Is this all there is to life? These are all the questions I had. Finally, the light came on. If I needed time to relax and enjoy myself; what about other mothers, caretakers, or busy women who need a break? Also during this quiet time, girl time, and me time, I rediscovered myself. Six months after this weekend, I started a weekend retreat so other women could experience the same thing I did. The name of this retreat is, Putting Me First. This is an annual weekend that I host in different cities. During the weekend, we relax, get pampered, have fun, and rediscover the hidden 'us'. The event starts on Thursday and we leave on Sunday. Can you imagine being by yourself or with your friends for a whole weekend? The time has come for women to stop existing and living for everyone but themselves. It's not selfish that we take moments for ourselves because if we aren't whole, then the people we take care of suffer. This book/planner is a tool to give you steps to intentionally taking time for yourself every day and not wait for a weekend away. You deserve more, you are more; now it's time to take action and live your life on purpose!

**Write down the following affirmations and say them out loud:
even if you do not believe them yet!**

1. I am fearfully and wonderfully made.

_____

2. I am the perfect woman.

_____

3. I wear my confidence like I wear my makeup.

_____

4. I discover new joys of living at every age.

_____

Week One
I'm Coming Out!

If you are close to a computer or your cell phone, Google the song, "I'm Coming Out" by Diana Ross. Before you press play, make sure, if you are at home or around someone else, to ask them to give you about
20 minutes by yourself with no interruptions. Turn on the song and turn it up where you can hear and feel it. Listen to the words and play it until it ends. Turn the song on again and dance! Let loose, dance, and lip sync with the song or sing out loud if you know it. I want you to have a full-out performance all by yourself. Act like you are in your own video... or that you are Diana Ross for that matter! (Only complete this task when you are in your own private space, not in public). One thing I do daily is sing and dance! Doing those things takes me to a happy place. My friend laughs at me often because I told her that any time one of my favorite songs come on, I pretend that I am in the video.

We women wear so many hats that we just have to let loose every once in a while. You should learn to take yourself to a happy place often. You cannot depend on someone else to do it.

"Dance like there's nobody watching,
Love like you'll never be hurt.
Sing like there's nobody listening,
And live like it's heaven on earth."

William W. Purkey

Describe how you felt once you completed your performance.

_____

_____

_____

_____

_____

_____

_____

_____

_____

Did you hesitate to turn the music on and dance? If so, why or why not?

_____

_____

_____

_____

_____

_____

_____

_____

_____

So what is your 'thing?' What do you do or say to put yourself in a good place?

_____

_____

_____

_____

_____

_____

_____

_____

_____

_____

_____

_____

If you don't have a 'thing', what do you think you would enjoy doing that would take less than 10 minutes a day to put you in a happy place or to help you forget about the worries of the day?

_____

_____

_____

_____

_____

_____

_____

Write down the following affirmations and say them out loud:

    1. I will intentionally make time for myself.

_____

    2. I will live my life with purpose.

_____

    3. I am in charge of making myself happy.

_____

    4. I have more than enough right now in my life.

_____

Week 2
Let's Get It, Let's Go!

Welcome to the best day of your life! You have chosen to make time for yourself. I'm glad you got started with the beginning of this book. Please do not do what I've done in the past and read the first part the book and not finish it! You owe it to yourself to make sure you are happy and whole. I don't know your situation; but I can tell you from experience that I spent at least five years of my life giving myself away to my husband, our daughter, friends, and family. Now while all those are awesome things to give yourself, what about you? Where do you fit in? Who were you before you started taking care of so many responsibilities? Take yourself back to the age of 18-25. What made you happy? Although you are grown now, what currently makes you happy? If you don't know, it's time to start finding out. Most women are born with a natural care taker instinct. We want to take care of everyone else but not ourselves. We matter too, and you need to know that. The bottom line is, if you aren't whole and in a happy place, no one you are taking care of or pouring yourself into will get your best. Please read and answer the following questions and statements. Be honest with your answers. This will be almost like your own diary.

What were you like between the age of 18-25 and what did you do for fun that you probably would still like to, but don't do or don't do often enough?

_____

_____

_____

_____

_____

_____

_____

_____

_____

_____

_____

_____

_____

_____

_____

_____

_____

When do you think you started putting the needs of others before your own?

_____

_____

_____

_____

_____

_____

_____

_____

_____

_____

_____

_____

_____

_____

_____

_____

_____

_____

Do you think there was something you can do to better balance your time to allow for the things that you like or that matter to you? If so, what?

_____

_____

_____

_____

_____

_____

_____

_____

_____

_____

_____

_____

_____

_____

_____

_____

_____

_____

_____

Write down the following affirmations and say them out loud:

1. I am investing in my mental health and clarity.

_____

2. My time is as important as anyone else's.

_____

3. It is not selfish to put myself on my schedule.

_____

4. My time is precious. I will not waste it.

_____

Week 3
Put Yourself on your Schedule

Please look at the calendar near the back of this book. You can also use your cell phone calendar if you need. Look over your schedule for the month and intentionally put yourself on it. You will be doing an activity in increments of 90 minutes at a time. If you have a hard time doing this, please start with one day a week. I have a family and sometimes they want my attention at the same time; so I tell them that I need time to myself. They know not to bother me within my 90-minute time frame. You may ask, well what do I do for 90 minutes? Revert back to the questions you answered already. It also may depend on your day. Some days, my brain feels like it's on overload. On those days, I put my cell phone on the charger in another room, get away from my family, go in the bedroom, lock the door and just lay there in silence. It sounds really simple but IT WORKS. My child and I had a talk a long time ago that sometimes mommy has had a long day and needs time to herself, even if my husband is not home. Most times you may feel that you are being selfish telling your family, friends or people you interact with every day that you need a break. After those 90 minutes, I can come back and deal with life again. In that 90 minutes, I'm not yelling at anyone, I'm in a great place for resting, and I'm recharged to handle the tasks at hand. By the end of this book, the goal is that you should have 90 minutes carved out for you at least three to four days a week, if not more. I hear you screaming through this book, "Yeah right!" But give it a try! You have to start somewhere and if you've gotten this far, you are headed in the right direction.

When you say "yes" to others, make sure you are not saying "no" to yourself.

Paulo Coelho

What day(s) did you choose for your 90 minutes of putting yourself first?

_____

_____

_____

_____

_____

_____

_____

_____

On those days, what are you going to do? If you haven't decided just yet, write down a list of things you would like to do during those times and start doing them.

_____

_____

_____

_____

_____

_____

_____

_____

_____

_____

_____

Week 4
Get the Girls Off the Floor!

GO GET MEASURED FOR A BRA!!! You are supposed to go at least once a year. THE RIGHT FITTING BRA MAKES YOUR OUTFIT LOOK GREAT!!! Just because you tried on a bra and you think it fits, doesn't mean you are wearing the right one. I'm going to be really honest, bras are expensive, especially for the size I wear; so I am not too anxious to go shopping for them. When I do go, I want to make sure I get the correct size and that it looks good under my shirt. If you are one of those ladies who gets fitted every year, great. If you haven't been to get sized or if it has been a while, put a bra fitting on your schedule. Getting fitted is free. You can google a local shop in your area. Most department stores will have someone who will measure you for free. Have fun! Make a full day of it!

What day have you scheduled to have your bra fitting?

_____

Were you wearing the correct size bra? _____

Did you purchase your correct size bra? _____

If you didn't purchase a bra, please make plans to do so within a month of your getting sized. When you look good, you feel good and your outfit ALWAYS starts with the correct undergarments.

"Having a good boyfriend is like having a good bra, it's all about support!"

Unknown

Week 5
Can I Take You Out Tonight?

In 2001, I enrolled one semester at a different college than I the one I originally attended. At the first college, I had several friends and I was hardly ever alone. I did almost everything with my friends. When I attended the other school, I knew only a few people from my hometown; but we hadn't hung out in several years so I was practically by myself there. Going to class by myself was not a problem; however, I had to eat lunch and go most other places by myself. It was a real wake up call. I thought everyone was looking at me because I was never with anyone. Even if I went with a few of the people I knew, I really didn't have a good time because I felt lost. During that year, I really got a chance to know who I was. I was able to really look in the mirror and get in touch with my feelings, my likes, and my dislikes. I can say that I am glad I had that experience early in life because I would probably be afraid to step outside of my comfort zone to do different things.

Fast forward to now, I've found that a lot of people will not go out in public by themselves because they think people are looking at them. When the fact is, NO ONE IS PAYING YOU ANY ATTENTION! It is all in your mind. So I am challenging you to take yourself out on a date! If you are used to going out on dates by yourself, great; you are going to do it again. If you aren't used to taking yourself out on a date, you are going to have the time of your life!!! You will be in awesome company because you will be with yourself.

Look at your calendar and figure out what day or evening you are free to go out. This particular date will consist of dinner and a movie. STOP FREAKING OUT!!!

I know going to dinner is one thing but the movies, especially in the evening by yourself makes you look pathetic, BUT TRUST ME, NO ONE IS LOOKING AT YOU... not unless you are looking cute! Below, I will walk you through your date night check list so you will be prepared. I guarantee you that once you take yourself out a few times, you will get more comfortable with who you are and you will be on the road to being a better you.

What date and time did you choose for your date? _____

What movie did you choose for your date? _____

What are your restaurant choices?

_____

Please choose your favorite restaurant-- one you haven't eaten at in a while or one you have been wanting to try. Hopefully, you will chose an awesome spot. There is nothing like looking cute in a nice place.
Choose a cute outfit. DO NOT GO OUT LOOKING FRUMPY. Act like you have a date with a man, a HOT MAN or with your husband if you are married. Hopefully your husband is hot too!

What outfit did you decide to go with? Describe what you are wearing from your top to your shoes:

_____

_____

_____

What movie did you see and did you like it?

_____

Write down your whole date experience. Don't leave out any details. Was it everything you dreamed it would be? Lol. No seriously, please talk about your date and how you felt going out by yourself.

_____

_____

_____

_____

_____

_____

_____

_____

_____

_____

_____

_____

_____

_____

_____

_____

_____

_____

"Date yourself. Take yourself out to eat. Don't share your popcorn at the movies with anyone. Stroll around an art museum alone. Fall in love with canvases. Fall in love with yourself."

Author Unknown

Write and say out loud these affirmations:

1. I am absolutely committed to being the person I was put on this earth to be.

_____

_____

2. I am aspiring to do great things. One by one, I will achieve them all.

_____

_____

3. My goal is my target and today I am on target.

_____

4.   I CAN! I WILL! And today I AM GOING TO DO IT!!

_____

Week 6
Vison Board Project

When I was in college, I pursued a degree in Apparel Merchandising and I hoped to become a buyer. I graduated and the next weekend started my career as an associate buyer for a large department store at their corporate office. I was there three months and I HATED IT! I had nightmares about it every night so when I was terminated, I cried, but not because I was leaving the job, I was wondering how I was going to pay my bills. I was engaged to be married in just two months. I was out of work for a total of three months and God blessed me with a job that I've been working in for over nine years. During the first two years of the job, I loved it because I was able to help people. I dressed up every day with a full face of makeup. After the first two years, I got pregnant and was out on maternity leave for only six weeks. I was sad to have to go back. I had to ask permission to be off from work or I had to be at work during a certain period of time during the week. I couldn't pick what days I wanted to work. For some, that's great, but I felt constrained. I wanted to get paid for what I enjoyed doing and go in when I wanted. The question was, what did I enjoy doing?

I didn't immediately determined what I wanted my life to look like; but later I used a vision board to help with that. I figured out what I loved about my life and also what I wanted my life to look like, including my body, my family and anyone else connected to me. I created my vision and now, you are going to do the same!

A vision board is used to help you concentrate and visualize your life goal(s).

This board will also represent whatever you want to be. You may ask, why would you need to do a vision board? I can tell you one of the problems with putting ourselves first is that often we tend to neglect our dreams and live for everyone else's. Now, we want to concentrate on your dreams, visions, and goals; then, work toward what will make you happy. Most times, it's the thing you love to do, and you would do it for free as it is the God-given ability you were born with.

Wouldn't it be a shame to leave this earth and not be happy and make money while doing it? YES, you can make money with your gift. We will get to that later on in the book. For now, just take one step at a time. Let's get your vision board done first.

"And the Lord answered me: "Write the vision; make it plain on tablets, so he may run who reads it."
Habakkuk 2:2

What you need:

- One foam cork board or large construction board (this board does not need to be thin)
- Scissors
- Glue Stick
- Magazines of your interest, dreams or goals
- Optional- Accessories such as markers, colored pencils, glitter, stickers, sticker quotes and letters, family pictures (that you don't mind cutting up or putting on the board) or colored or design paper.

Step 1:

When I did my first vision board, I did it with a couple of my friends. We made a girl's night out of it with dinner and conversation about our goals and aspirations. You may not want to share this experience with others; that's fine. With someone else or alone, you will have all weekend to complete your project. Please allow yourself at least one to four hours to complete your vision board. Go to a quiet space where you can concentrate on yourself.

Step 2:

Create a relaxing atmosphere. For example, you can light candles and put on some relaxing or upbeat music you like. Before you get started, take a minute to think about your dreams and goals. This board should reflect what you want your life to look like.

Step 3:

Cut out images from magazines that represent the life you want to live. For example, if you want to become a singer, you might cut out photos of singers you love or admire. Or if you want to find a husband, you may clip pictures of what you want your mate to look like, or of happy couples. You don't have to use photos, you can also cut out quotes or phrases you like. There is no "right way" to add your images to the board.

Use your markers or paint to write your personal or favorite quotes on your vision board.

Step 4:

Display your vision board somewhere you will see it every day and feel inspired! If you like, you can also frame your vision board and hang it on your wall.

For a visual, please refer to the YouTube video:
How to Make a Vision Board by Dr. Rose Moten

Please write about your Vision Board experience in detail. What is your vision for your life?

_____

_____

_____

_____

_____

_____

_____

_____

_____

_____

_____

_____

_____

_____

_____

_____

_____

_____

_____

_____

Write and say out loud these affirmations:

1. I will invest time and money on my skin.

_____

2. I will try my BEST to drink half of my body weight in water each day.

_____

3. I will purchase and use my skin care system on a regular basis.

_____

4. I will make sure my lips are always exfoliated and moisturized.

_____

Week 7
You Can't Take Your Face Off!

Along with getting older and having my child, my skin changed drastically. For years I've always LOVED to shop and get cute clothes. I also LOVE makeup but I knew if I didn't get my skin together, it didn't matter what makeup I put on, my face would look a mess. I decided to invest in my skin because I wanted to feel confident enough to go out without a full face of makeup. In 2013, I started shopping around for skin care products. I needed someone who really knew what they were doing. I didn't want skin care that had a lot of harsh chemicals in it and I also wanted a system that worked together to take care of everything I needed. I finally found an awesome skincare regimen that I am happy with. It's not too cheap but not too terribly expensive either. I only have to get the system every four to five months. Think about all the clothes you buy; you may lose or gain weight. Either way, you have to buy clothes. But your skin is the only skin you have and you shouldn't take it for granted. You can take off your clothes, but you can't take off your skin/face. Take care of it. If you have a skin care regimen already, keep doing what you're are doing! Go girl! If not, keep reading.

Your assignment this week is to shop around for different skin care products if you don't have something you are using already. DO NOT shop on your own. Please talk to a consultant--someone who has been with their company for more than two years and is successful (my opinion.) I've been with BeautiControl with consultant Yahrasiel Colbert since 2013 and I love them and her. So if you want to start there, I think it's a good place. Invest in your face!

Write down a list of different skin care companies you are thinking of trying.

"The more you take care of your skin, the less makeup you have to wear."
Demi Moore

Write and say out loud these affirmations:

1. I will not let what happened in my past affect my future.

_____

2. I am not the bad things that happened to me.

_____

3. I will forgive myself for wrong choices I have made.

_____

4. I am ready to move forward with my life

_____

Week 8
New Beginnings

I am adopted and grew up an only child in a perfectly, imperfect middleclass household. I was molested twice, was a HUGE LIAR, was VERY promiscuous, and was addicted to pornography. I had two abortions by two different men, smoked weed, drank, and slept with a married man. That sounds like a lot of things to go through. Maybe it doesn't, depending on your story. But one thing we have in common is that WE ALL HAVE A STORY! I'm sure you have asked yourself at one time or another about why bad things happened to you, or why you made the decisions you have made when you knew better. You have asked why did all this have to happen. You may not believe in God, but the ONLY answer that I can honestly give you is that if you have not accepted Jesus as your Lord and Savior, you do not stand a chance against an enemy (the devil) who DOES NOT want you to succeed or have a positive future. If you stop and think about it, most bad things that have happened to you, happened in your childhood. The enemy comes to kill, steal and destroy your life and the people in or around you. He wants to cause a stronghold on your life--something from which you can't recover. The things we go through are meant to empower us and help free someone else from their past. I can freely tell you about my past because I'm no longer bound by it.

The enemy wants you to hold on to those things and not tell anyone because he wants you to feel like you are the only person who has gone through these things. BUT THE DEVIL IS A LIAR! You live your life for you but you also live your life to come to an expected place and to help free other people who may be going through your same situation. You may not believe in Jesus or the devil. But I'm sure something resonates with you in a few things I have said. We have done all these things but now it's time to deal with the things you probably don't want to talk about. It's important to address them so we can heal and move on.

"Forgiving isn't something you do for someone else. It's something you do for yourself. It's saying you're not important enough to have a stranglehold on me. It's saying, you don't get to trap me in the past. I am worthy of a future."
Jodi Picoult

Week 8 Continued
Burn Baby Burn

On a separate sheet of paper write about all the bad things that have happened in your life or the bad decisions you have made. Write them out in detail. If you need more than one sheet that's fine but get EVERYTHING OUT! Empty all of your thoughts--even the ones you have suppressed. After you've finished, get a large cup of water and a lighter. Take the paper(s) outside somewhere there is concrete, or something that won't catch fire. Set the paper(s) on fire and let it burn! Pour the water on it once it's burnt to a crisp but MAKE SURE YOU PUT THE FIRE OUT BEFORE YOU BURN SOMETHING OTHER THAN THE PAPER. If you can't do it, please get some help. If you are reading this book with a friend, maybe you can do it together for support. Once the paper(s) are in wet ashes, yell out loud, I AM FREE! I RELEASE ALL THESE HURTS AND I FORGIVE MYSELF! I AM MOVING FORWARD WITH MY LIFE! I WILL START LIVING MY BEST LIFE RIGHT NOW! From this point on, do not live in the past. Press toward the future and everything that's in it.

Talk about your experience of writing out your past and burning it. How did you feel? Did you want to do it? Are you glad you did it?

_____

_____

_____

_____

_____

_____

_____

_____

_____

_____

_____

_____

_____

_____

_____

_____

_____

_____

What steps have you taken or are thinking about taking to move forward to have a better life?

_____

_____

_____

_____

_____

_____

_____

_____

_____

_____

_____

_____

_____

_____

_____

_____

_____

_____

_____

_____

_____

_____

Write and say out loud these affirmations:

1. I will make time to relax so I can function better during the week.

_____

2. I will pamper myself on purpose.

_____

3. Pampering is a way to show myself love.

_____

4. Pampering myself will boost my self-esteem and confidence.

_____

Week 9
An Evening of Pampering Yourself

I know, I know, I KNOW! You have heard a million times to pamper yourself. But you need to be intentional in consistently doing it and enjoying it. Taking a shower or bath does not have to be a rushed experience. I suggest you take at least two nights a week and take a long hot bath or shower. Light candles, turn on your favorite music, and have some sparkling cider or a cup of hot relaxation tea... sorry girls, I don't drink. Lol. Below are a couple of detox baths that will have you relax while pulling the toxins out of your body. After you get out of the tub, moisturize well and just lay there. If you live by yourself... THIS IS PERFECT!!! If you have a family, please explain to your mate, if you have one that you are taking some me time and he is on baby-sitting duty. If you are a single mother, the best time pamper time is when your family is sleeping. This is the ultimate time to relax and not think too hard. You deserve it. Pampering yourself is self-love. It will boost your self-esteem and your self-confidence; and that will eventually show other people how to treat you.

"My evening really begins when I take a long, hot bath. I light a candle, and I turn on the news and try to catch up. It's when I can breathe from the day to the night, and that means a lot to me."
Vera Wang

Detox Bath Ideas and Recipes

Epsom Salt Detox– Epsom salt draws out toxins while you are relaxing in a hot bath. Epsom salt is said to be able to help with the circulatory system as well as improving nerve functions. Taking a regular Epsom salt bath is a great way to improve your health and well-being.

~2 cups of Epsom salt

Apple Cider Vinegar Detox– Apple Cider Vinegar can be taken both internally and used externally to treat a number of conditions. It helps with conditions like arthritis and gout, as well as anything else caused by inflammation. This is a good bath to take if you feel you need to sweat the toxins out, and it also helps you get to sleep without lying awake with a wandering mind.

~1-2 C of raw Apple cider vinegar added to warm to hot water.

Write and say out loud these affirmations:

1. My past happened to make me stronger.

_____

2. I will not let the bad things that happened to me in the past keep me from being happy.

_____

_____

3. The past is gone. I only live in the present.

_____

4. I forgive myself so that I can forgive others.

_____

Week 10
Getting to Know You, Getting to know all about you

This next assignment will be pretty lengthy. I want you to go all the way back to your first memory as a child up to where you are now in your adult life. Write about everything that happened in your life--good and bad--and how you think it has shaped your life as an adult. Also talk about different steps you can take to be a better you, and change some things about yourself that you know you need to change.

_____

_____

_____

_____

_____

_____

_____

_____

_____

_____

_____

_____

_____

"Holding on to anything is like holding on to your breath. You will suffocate. The only way to get anything in the physical universe is by letting go of it. Let go and it will be yours forever."

Deepak Chopra

Week 11
Essentially Yours

Essential oil has been around for many years and over the course of the past five years, they have grown even more popular. These oils can be used for a number of things such as possible help with relaxation, weight loss, and positive feelings. Lavender oil is my favorite for relaxation when I take baths. I run the bath water as hot as I can get it and add four to six drops. I take deep breaths while I relax in the tub. Once I get out of the tub, I rub with lotion, put on my favorite gown, and sleep like a baby. Below are some of the other favorite essential oils I use and love. If you haven't used any of them, remember, try something new!

Lemon – May help with bad breath, improves digestion, relieves cough , calms stomach, relieves nausea, and promotes weight loss.

Lavender –May help with sleep, nervous system, acne, pain , blood circulation, and immune system.

Week 12
Selfie Account

I'm sure you have always heard that you need to invest in yourself. Yes, everyone should have a savings account but no one has ever told you to have a selfie account. This account is JUST FOR YOU! So you may ask, what do you do with it? You do whatever you want with it that will give you a better quality of life and will make you happy! So how much do you spend? I'm glad you asked. You may say that you don't have enough money to invest in yourself, but you really can't afford not to invest in yourself. Your life and the ones who care about you and the ones you care for depend on you, so you should at the least save $25-$50 a month, but I would lean more toward $50. If you think about it, you blow that or more each month and don't really have anything to show for it. Let this money have a purpose--you. I have a separate account of my own at another bank; the money comes out of my check and it is just for me.

"Your body will be around a lot longer than that expensive handbag. Invest in yourself."
Unknown

Write and say out loud these affirmations:

1. I accept that I did the best I could at the time with what I knew.

_____

2. I let go of all self-judgement and self -sabotage.

_____

3. I am capable of loving all of who I am.

_____

4. I am taking small steps to work on my growth.

_____

Week 13
IT WILL KILL YOU

I have had people in my past take money from me, sleep with my past boyfriend, lie, and gossip about me. I also had a guy I was dating say he wasn't able to have children when I told him I was pregnant with his child; I obtained an abortion with no help from anyone. I was also molested by a friend of the family. I saw things in my childhood growing up that could make me very resentful but what would that help? A lot of times, different situations happen in our lives to literally kill us emotionally, and harm current and future relationships; or to keep us from having loving and positive relationships. I am 37 years old and I still find it hard to talk about some of the things that happened in my past, which others did to me. Why would I let this affect my having a good quality of life or having great relationships or a promising future? Are you letting something hold you back from being the best person you can be? If so, PLEASE LET IT GO! Yes, it is easier said than done. But look at it this way. Think about the WORST THING that has happened to you and the person who did it. Do you think this person has put his/her life on hold thinking about what they did to you? I'll give you a minute. The answer is NO! They have gone on living their life and you are still holding onto being angry and talking or thinking about what happened in the past. Heaven forbid that your offender is dead and you are still holding onto these hurts!

These people have literally moved on and are no longer thinking about what they did to you, so why are you still letting it affect you? As TD Jakes says, "Forgiveness is for you, not the other person." You have to live with the fact that you may never get an apology for what happened in the past but when you forgive them and move on, life is so much better. So today, I charge you to forgive your offenders, if you haven't already, and move on. Jesus actually helped me get free from past hurts. I just said out loud that I thank the Lord for helping me release past hurts and thanked him for peace concerning my situations. It didn't happen overnight but the more I spoke it, the more peace I received and I've moved on with my life.

Week 14
Hobby

I have always LOVED hosting events and giving to people to make them happy. I was doing this for free by hosting family reunions and get-togethers for my friends. As I stated earlier, I went on a short trip to Atlanta with a friend and spent some time alone and with her. During that weekend, I decided that I would host an event for women to get together once a year in a different state for a full weekend. During this weekend, the attendees would be pampered, have fun, shop, and have empowerment sessions. To be honest, I didn't start the women's weekend thinking about making money. I started it because there was a need for women to relax and get away from their busy lives for a while. Six months later, Putting Me First: The Ultimate Women's Getaway Weekend was born. After that weekend, I knew I was onto something and thought, "I can make some money from my hobby." I knew I wanted to make this trip affordable and I wasn't out to get rich but it just made sense to do something I loved and make some extra money doing it.

What is the hobby you like to do for fun that might be able to make money for you? Or what is a hobby that you used to do that you said you would pick back up but haven't yet? You don't have to start a hobby just to make money; it can just bring you joy and a better quality of life. Another example is, I started getting bored with my job. Once I started my "hobby," I was more content at my job and in my life at home. My family started seeing that I was happier and wasn't complaining about not having anything to do. I challenge you today to find a hobby or pick back up a hobby so your quality of life or bank account can be better.

What hobby do you have or would like to find to possibly allow you to have fun or make money? Or what are you currently working on to make money but haven't fully developed yet? What steps can you take to potentially turn this into extra money?

_____

_____

_____

_____

_____

_____

_____

_____

_____

_____

_____

_____

_____

_____

_____

_____

_____

"Persistence. Perfection. Patience. Power. Prioritize your passion. It keeps you sane."
Edith Sitwell

Week 15
Staycation

A staycation is time you spend at home and participate in leisurely activities within driving distance, sleeping in your own bed or at a hotel at night. You will make day trips to local tourist sites, swimming venues, or engage in fun activities such as horseback riding, hiking, or visiting museums, new restaurants etc.

Ladies, at this point, you should be ready to go off for a whole night BY YOURSELF!!! The idea is for you to have a whole day and night by yourself. Get up and have an awesome breakfast and if you want to, take another day to yourself. Please put some thought into your daily excursions and the hotel where you will stay. DO NOT! I REPEAT DO NOT STAY AT ANYONE'S HOME. The point of this staycation is for you to treat yourself to an awesome day and a nice hotel because YOU ARE WORTH IT. Do your research and try to incorporate places you have never been, along with places you love that you haven't been to in a while.

"Stay Sane and Staycate."
Unknown

Write down a list of places you want to visit and possibly pencil them in on the calendar in this book:_____

_____

_____

You may have to come back to this question after you have completed your first Staycation. Please DO NOT wait too long to schedule and go to your destination. Describe your whole experience with your staycation trip. What did you do? Where did you go? How did you feel? Don't leave anything out!

_____

_____

_____

_____

_____

_____

_____

_____

_____

_____

_____

_____

_____

Week 16
Chat and Chew

Until a while ago, my friend would always say, "All you do is talk about your husband and child all the time." At first, I was offended, but often when you get offended, you are being told the truth. I went home and thought about what she said and she was right. I had no friends with whom I could hang out. It was literally just me and my family. I forgot how to go out and have fun with my girlfriends. Since college, I had none. Oh that is so sad. I also remember when I first met the friend mentioned above, I told her I didn't want any friends. How mean was that? When in actuality, I was really hurting from past friendships and I didn't really know how to make new friends or how to open up so that was my best defense mechanism. Well a few years later, she is my good friend and we hang out all the time. Just think, if I hadn't opened up to the possibility of new friendships, I would still be at home being bored. So long story short, your story may not be my story but if you have friends that you haven't hung out with in a while, PLEASE make some time for them. Have a girl's night or day for yourself . Go get manicures and massages; or have lunch, brunch, game night, movie night, or a vision board party. The list goes on. I think you should get together with your friend(s) at least quarterly.

"If you hear any noise, it ain't the boys. It's a Ladies Night, ah-ha. Gonna step out Ladies Night, steppin' out Ladies Night."

Kool And The Gang

Ladies Night/Day Preparation:

Ladies Night/Day Theme:

_____

Date: _____

Time: _____

Invitation List:

_____

_____

_____

_____

_____

_____

_____

_____

_____

_____

_____

Explain dress attire if any:

_____

_____

_____

What quarterly date did you come up with for your ladies get together? _____.Write it down, but also put it on the calendar near the back of this book.

Talk about your girl's night/day. Explain it from start to finish and how it made you feel.

_____

_____

_____

_____

_____

_____

_____

_____

_____

_____

_____

_____

_____

_____

_____

BONUS
You didn't even see it coming

Get in a quiet space, preferable in your home before you go to bed. Be quiet for about five minutes. During this time, clear your mind and take several deep breathes. Talk out loud about your current concerns. Maybe you need a better job, or another home. Just talk out loud about the things you need and the things you want to improve in your life. Basically, talk like you are talking to your best friend but talk about it in detail. This will seem like a one-sided conversation, but it isn't. When I have problems, I say all of them out loud to God because He's my best friend. He knows what's going on before you even say anything. He is just waiting for you to talk to Him about it so he can assist you. Now, if you don't believe in Jesus, I'm just asking you to try Him. Talk to Him about your problems out loud and wait for His response. And even if you are saved and believe in Jesus, you can still do this. I talk to Him all the time. Jesus is not only my Lord, He's my homie! He understands me better than anyone because His Dad made me! It is His will that everyone be saved but not everyone answers that call as He is a God of free will. That alone makes me happy. He doesn't force Himself on us. What I can say, since I've accepted Jesus Christ as the Lord and Savior of my life, my bad days are better with Him than without Him. I also wouldn't be able to write this book about feeling good about myself and my life. If you could only get a glimpse of how He feels about you and who He said you are, you would be on cloud 9 every day!

You should have already talked to Jesus at this point so I will end this book by saying I hope that you do not depart this life without being saved or recommitting your life to Jesus Christ. The biggest lie the devil ever told me was that I can't have fun and be saved. As my pastor always says, "If I knew then what I know now, I would have been saved 25 years ago." That is a very true statement.

And please believe me when I say there is NOTHING that you have EVER done that will keep Jesus from loving you and prevent your being saved.

If you are interested in being saved, please say the statement below out loud. Start searching for a Word church that is Bible-based and believes in the five-fold ministry. Get involved in serving. If you aren't sure what church to attend, ask God to lead you while you are visiting churches.

Prayer: Jesus, please forgive me of my sins. I repent of all my sins right now. I believe that Jesus Christ died on the cross for all of my sins. I accept Him right now as Lord and Savior of my life. Amen.

"Ask and it will be given to you; seek and you will find; knock and the door will be opened to you."
Matthew 7:7

How did you feel about calming yourself and talking to Jesus? Has anything good happened as the result of your talking to him?

_____

_____

_____

_____

_____

_____

_____

_____

_____

_____

_____

_____

_____

_____

_____

_____

_____

_____

_____

_____

_____

Use these calendars to schedule events in your life.

Month_____   Year _____

Add the number of days depending on the month/year as everyone will start this book at different times

Sun	Mon	Tue	Wed	Thu	Fri	Sat

Month_____   **Year** _____

Sun	Mon	Tue	Wed	Thu	Fri	Sat

Month_____ **Year** _____

Sun	Mon	Tue	Wed	Thu	Fri	Sat

Month_____   **Year** _____

Sun	Mon	Tue	Wed	Thu	Fri	Sat

Month_____   **Year** _____

Sun	Mon	Tue	Wed	Thu	Fri	Sat

Month_____ **Year** _____

Sun	Mon	Tue	Wed	Thu	Fri	Sat

Month_____   **Year** _____

Sun	Mon	Tue	Wed	Thu	Fri	Sat

Month_____ **Year** _____

Sun	Mon	Tue	Wed	Thu	Fri	Sat

Month_____   **Year** _____

Sun	Mon	Tue	Wed	Thu	Fri	Sat

Month_____ **Year** _____

Sun	Mon	Tue	Wed	Thu	Fri	Sat

Month_____ **Year** _____

Sun	Mon	Tue	Wed	Thu	Fri	Sat

Month_____   **Year _____**

Sun	Mon	Tue	Wed	Thu	Fri	Sat

Month_____ Year _____

Add number to the days depending on the month/year as everyone will start this book at different times

Sun	Mon	Tue	Wed	Thu	Fri	Sat

Month_____   Year _____

Sun	Mon	Tue	Wed	Thu	Fri	Sat

Month_____ **Year** _____

Sun	Mon	Tue	Wed	Thu	Fri	Sat

Month_____   **Year** _____

Sun	Mon	Tue	Wed	Thu	Fri	Sat

Month_____ **Year** _____

Sun	Mon	Tue	Wed	Thu	Fri	Sat

Month_____ **Year** _____

Sun	Mon	Tue	Wed	Thu	Fri	Sat

Month_____ **Year** _____

Sun	Mon	Tue	Wed	Thu	Fri	Sat

Month_____ **Year** _____

Sun	Mon	Tue	Wed	Thu	Fri	Sat

Month_____ **Year** _____

Sun	Mon	Tue	Wed	Thu	Fri	Sat

Month_____   **Year** _____

Sun	Mon	Tue	Wed	Thu	Fri	Sat

Month_____ **Year** _____

Sun	Mon	Tue	Wed	Thu	Fri	Sat

Month_____   **Year** _____

Sun	Mon	Tue	Wed	Thu	Fri	Sat

Month_____ **Year** _____

Sun	Mon	Tue	Wed	Thu	Fri	Sat

Journal

This portion of the book is for your journal. Before you go to sleep at night, write about your day, what happened and the thoughts you had and how you can make tomorrow better. Happy writing!

_____

_____

_____

_____

_____

_____

_____

_____

_____

_____

_____

_____

_____

_____

_____

_____

_____

_____

_____

_____

_____

_____

Made in the USA
Monee, IL
25 January 2022

89670092R00138